A Step-by-Step Visual Guide to WooCommerce

By Mandy Oviatt

Edited by Lyle Dillie.

Published in the United States of America

First Printing, 2014

ISBN:9781500814366

Desert Sea Design
12409 W. Indian School Rd Suite
A102
Avondale, AZ 85392

www.Desertseadesign.com

WooCommerce is a WordPress plugin designed to help businesses sell their products to customers easily *and* to let customers order with ease. With WooCommerce, you can easily add new products, edit existing products, and manage orders.

With WooCommerce, you can even sell variations of products. WooCommerce can also show sales reports, allow you to manage tax and shipping. With this booklet, you will be able to manage your products, coupons, and orders through WooCommerce.

Disclaimer: this WooCommerce, like many other web applications, is constantly changing and your actual experiences with the app might vary from the pictures portrayed in this guide. info@desertesadesign.com.

4

Table of Contents:

Getting Started

After you have installed your WooCommerce plugin, you can use WooCommerce by logging in to your WordPress Account:

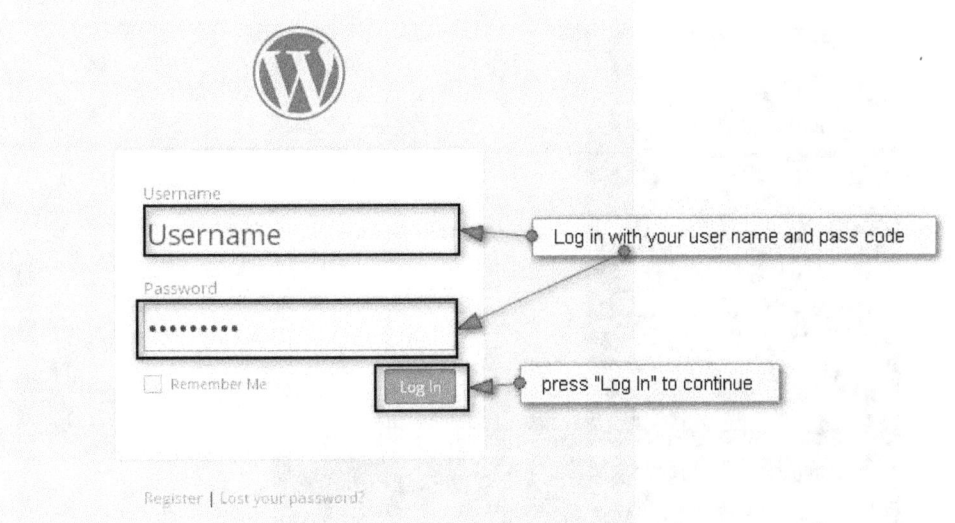

- Enter your Username and Pass code from yourwebpage.com/login screen.
- Press "log in" to log in.

Once you've logged in, navigate to the left hand side of your screen, to the dashboard.

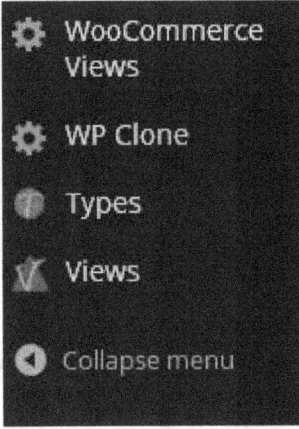

You will see a link in your Dashboard called "WooCommerce" Click on this link, and you will see a quick link to a variety of WooCommerce Options.

The options can show in one of two ways:

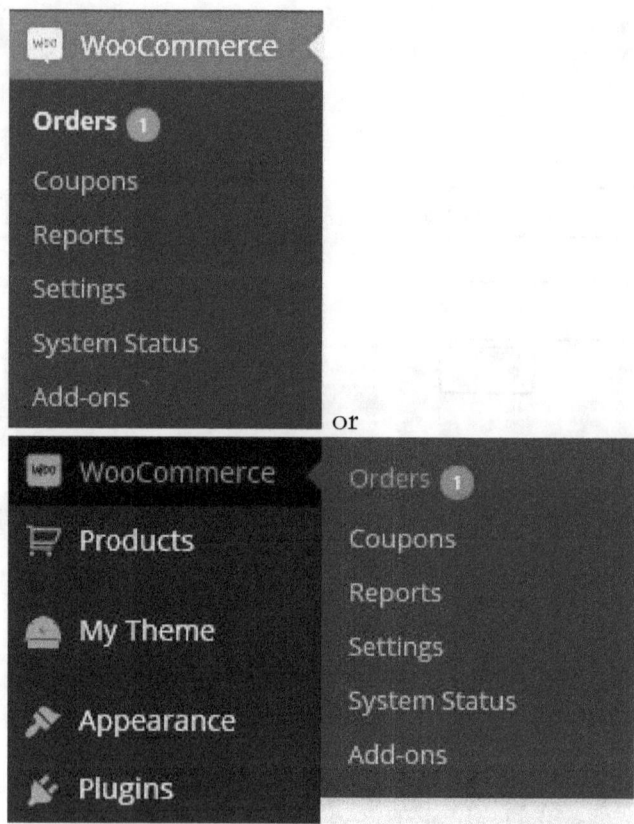

or

Either option will send you to your Woo Commerce to build your online store.

From here, you can navigate to your WooCommerce Plugin and begin building your Online store.

Now that you've logged in to your site and have found the WooCommerce plugin, you can begin to add products to your site.

Managing your Products with WooCommerce

In this section, we will discuss how to *add products, edit products,* and *manage products* in WooCommerce.

Adding New Products through WooCommerce.

To add your products in your WooCommerce store, log in to your WordPress account and navigate to the Dashboard. Your Dashboard will have a menu called "products."

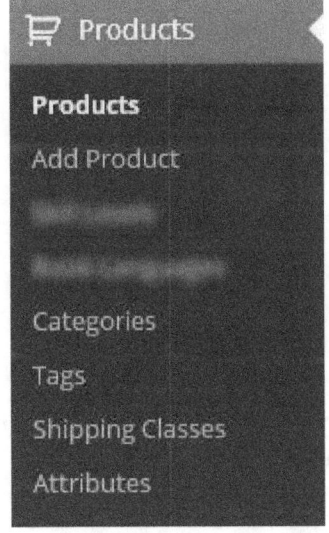

From this menu, you will add and edit your products on your WordPress Site.

To Add a product, select "Add a Product."

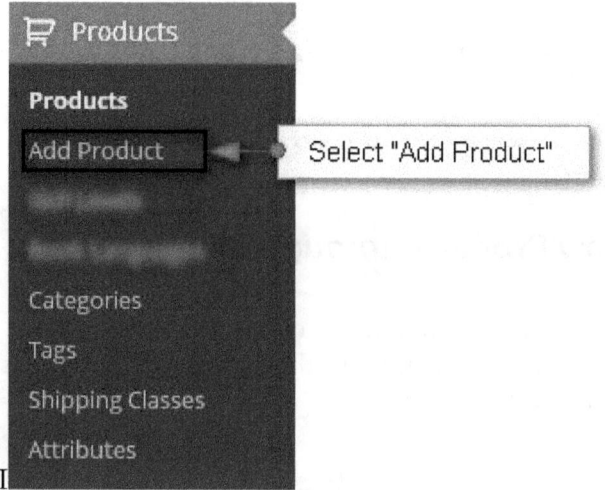

You will be navigated to this screen:

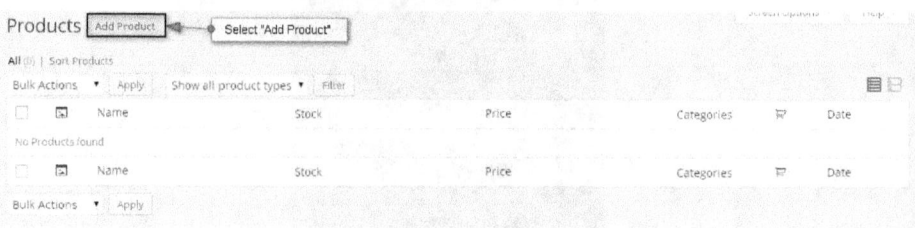

Click "Add Product" to begin adding a product.

Once you begin adding your products, there are a number of options you can use with each product.

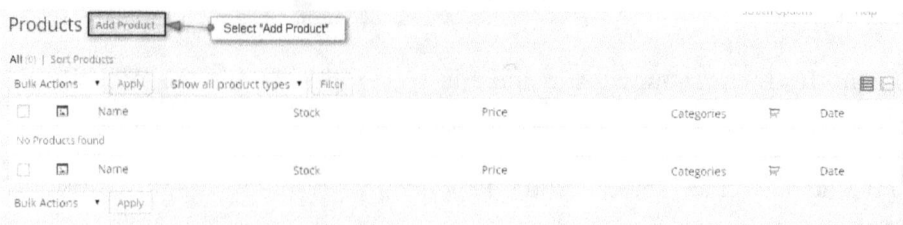

First, name your product and describe it.

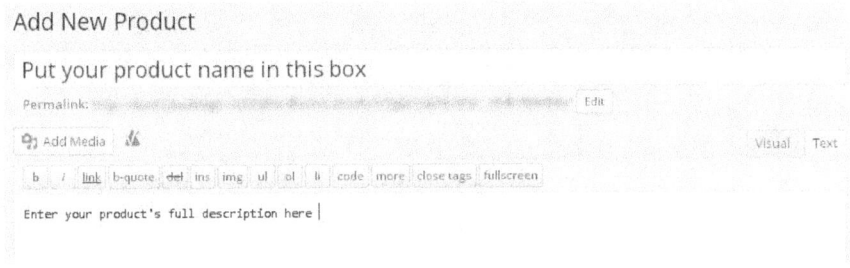

Enter your product's name and full description. The name and description are two things that your customers will see and what will help your customers learn about your amazing products.

Product Type

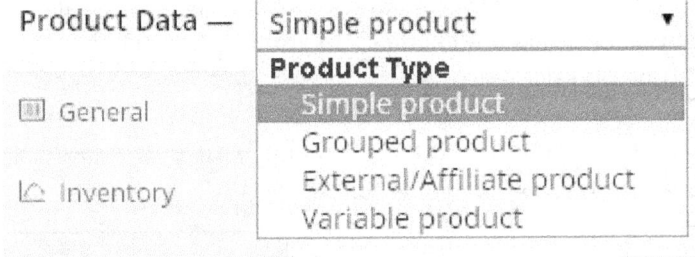

In this drop-down box, you can edit specific product data if you are selling external, grouped, or variable products. The default is "simple product." Unless you have advanced inventory options, leave this box on that default option.

General Tab:

After entering product name, description, and checking product type, you may want to edit the price and important information about your products.

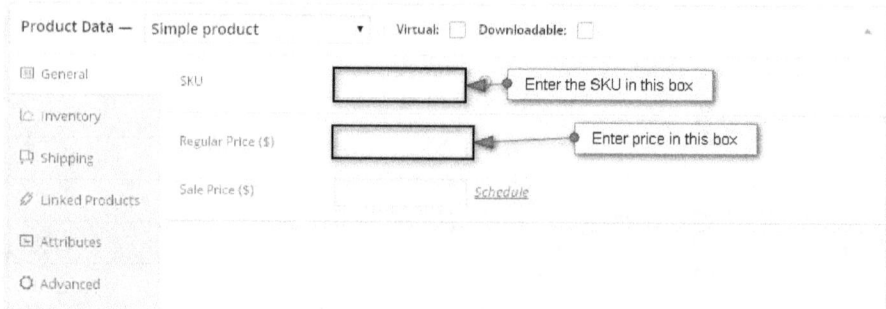

Enter the SKU in the SKU box and the Price in the box marked "regular price."

Sale Price

If you wish to schedule a sale for your products, you may enter the sale price in the bottom box and select "schedule" to apply applicable dates for your products to be on sale.

In the *Product Data* section, section, you may also check the boxes to select virtual or downloadable products (discussed on page 10).

Pricing and product SKUs are general information and are required for your customers to make their purchases. You may also want to include more specific information that you cannot find in the product data tabs. For this, you will want to **Add a Custom Field.**

Adding Custom Fields (like ISBNs).

Next, you can add custom fields to your product. These fields can help you list things like product number, publication date, or ISBN.
First scroll down to the section below "**Product Data**," labeled "Custom Fields.

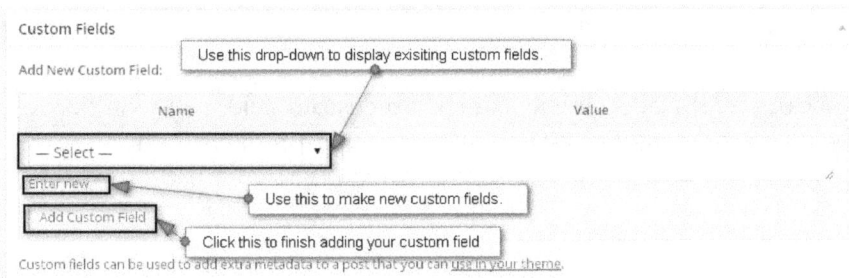

"Enter New" will allow you to create custom fields. Once you've selected "Enter New" you can begin adding your new custom Field:

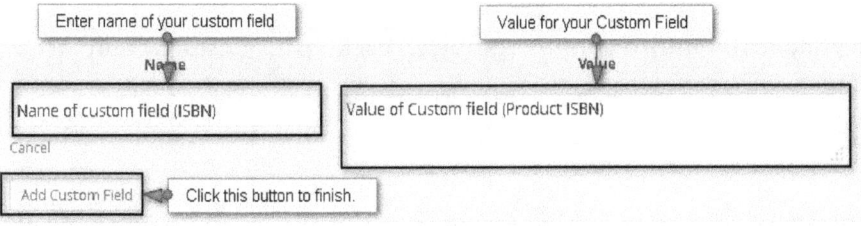

- Under "Name" enter the name of your new custom field (for example, ISBN)
- Under "Value" enter the value of that custom field (for instance, product ISBN)
- Select "Add Custom Field" to complete your custom field.

The excellent thing about WooCommerce custom fields is that once you've added a custom field to a single product, you don't have to add it as a new custom field for future products. Simply click the drop-down menu to select your existing custom field.

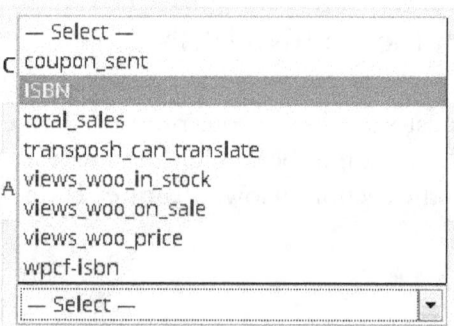

As you can see, ISBN is already added as a custom field, so I won't have to make a new custom field for ISBNS for other products. I will simply have to select "ISBN" in the drop down menu then add that information in the field.

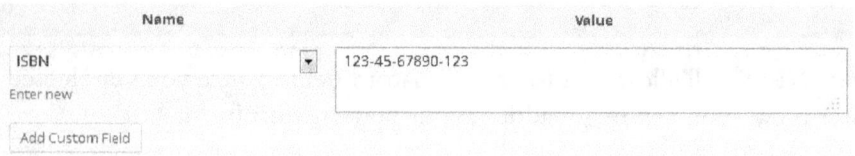

Once the ISBN information is complete, click "Add Custom Field" to complete the process.

Adding Downloadable Products to your site

Through WooCommerce, adding a downloadable product (such as an e-book) is simple!

- First, follow all the steps to **Add A Product** (page 5 of this workbook).
- Next, when you go to the Product Data portion of the process, check the box that says "Downloadable."

Once you've selected downloadable, scroll down. An extra portion has been added to the "Product Data" section of your screen.

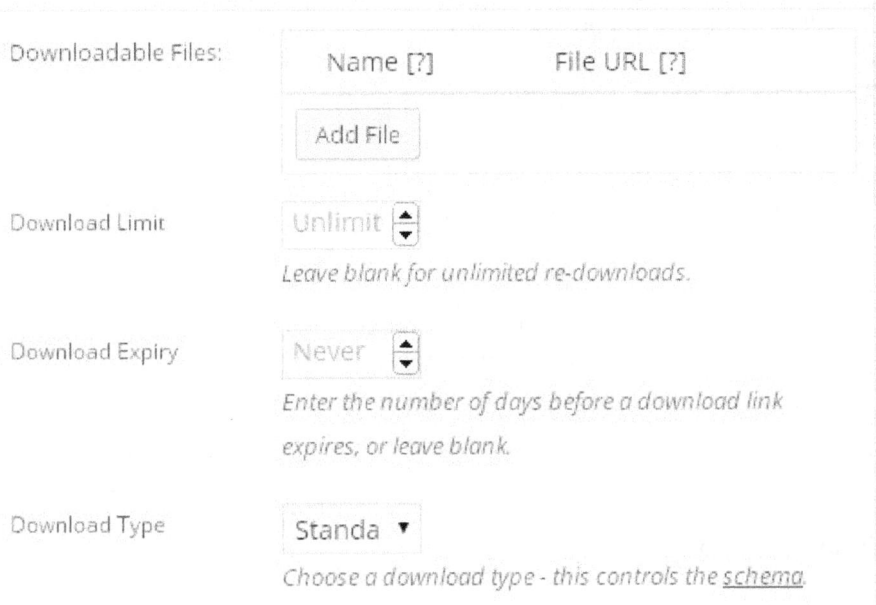

This section is where you Add the Download and Manage Download properties.

To add the downloadable file, click on the "Add File" Box.

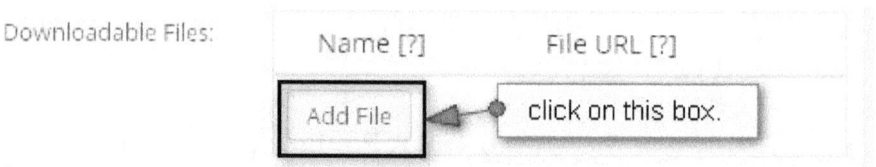

Next, you will see a place to Name your File and Upload the File.

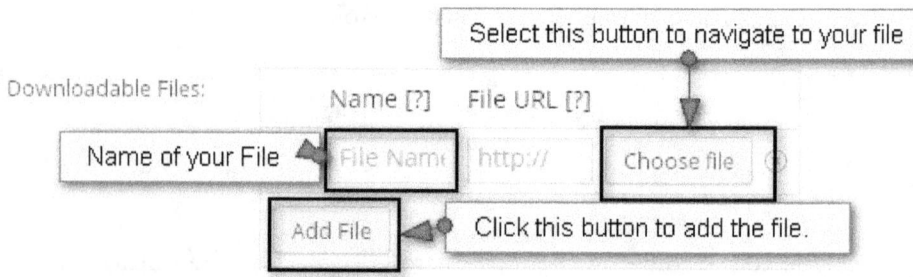

First, click the "Choose File" insert your file.

You will be directed to your WordPress Media Library:

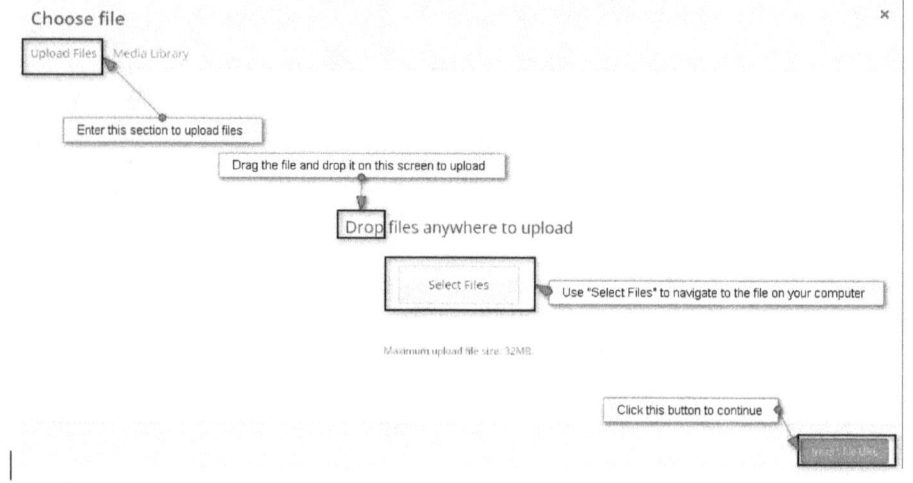

To add the file, go to "Upload Files"

From here you can either "Drag and Drop" your files to this screen or navigate to the file on your computer.

WordPress will take a few moments to upload your file, during which a blue status bar will appear to show the upload process. When the file is completely uploaded, the file will appear in your media library and the "Insert the URL" button will be selectable.

When that happens, click the "Insert the URL" button to proceed.

Once you've selected the file, click "Add File" to add the file to the product.

Before you finish the "downloadable product section," make sure that you take a look at the following portion of the downloadable products menu.

This section controls the amount of re-downloads and expiration of downloads your customer receives. Leave them blank if you want your customer to have unlimited downloads or unlimited time before the download expires.

Download Type allows you to select "standard", "Application/software" or "Music." Unless your product is music or a computer application, leave this blank.

Product Categories

If you have products that are similar, you can add categories to your online catalogue.
Categories are an excellent way for customers to find similar products and can increase sales in those like-products.

The Product Category widget is on the right hand side of your WordPress administrator screen.

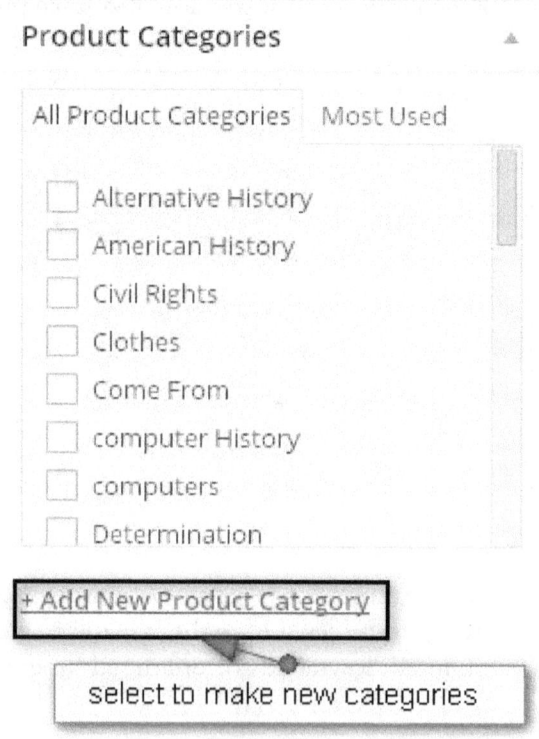

To add a new product category, click the "Add New Product Category Link and enter the category in the box:

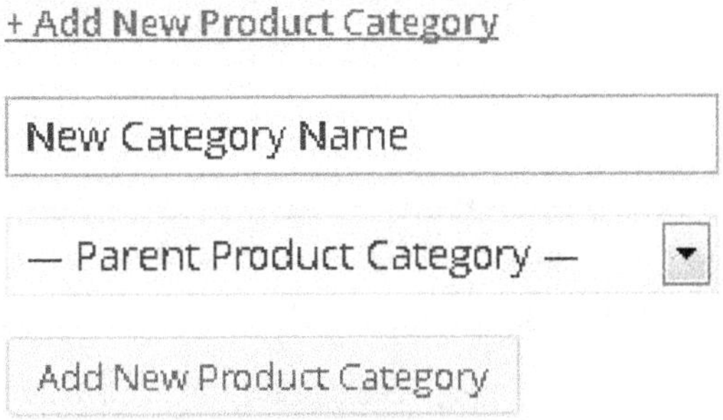

+ Add New Product Category

New Category Name

— Parent Product Category — ▾

Add New Product Category

Press the "Add New Product Category to finish adding the Category.

Note: If you want to place this new category in a Sub Category (for instance "Physics" under a "Science" category," first add the new "Parent Category" using the steps above.

Then add the Sub category, and find the "Parent Category" in the drop-down menu.

Adding Product Images for your WooCommerce Products

While creating your Product, it is important to include an image of your products so that your customers know what product they are purchasing. Otherwise, your product screen will not demonstrate an accurate image of what your customer is purchasing.

To add an image, first look to the right sidebar of your Product page. You will find widgets called "Product Gallery" and "Product Image"

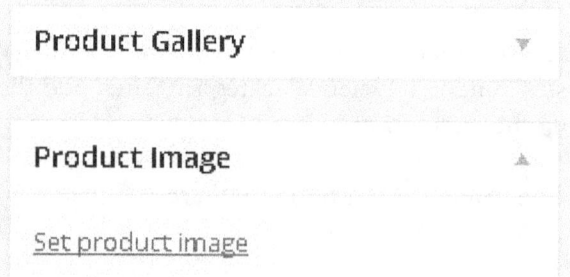

Click on the link "Set product image" to continue.

You will be directed to this screen:

From here you have two options to upload the images. Both options are fairly similar, but have the same outcome.

If you are directed to the tab labeled "Media Library," you will see all existing photos in your WordPress library. If the image is not yet uploaded, click on the "Upload files" tab.

Next, you can choose to **Drop your Files** or **Select files**.
If you choose to "Select files," a Navigation screen will pop up.

- Navigate to find your desired image.
- When you find your desired image, select it
- Press "Open image"

WordPress will begin to upload your image. A blue status bar will appear on your screen, showing the upload progress. When the upload is complete, press the "Set Product Image" to set the image.

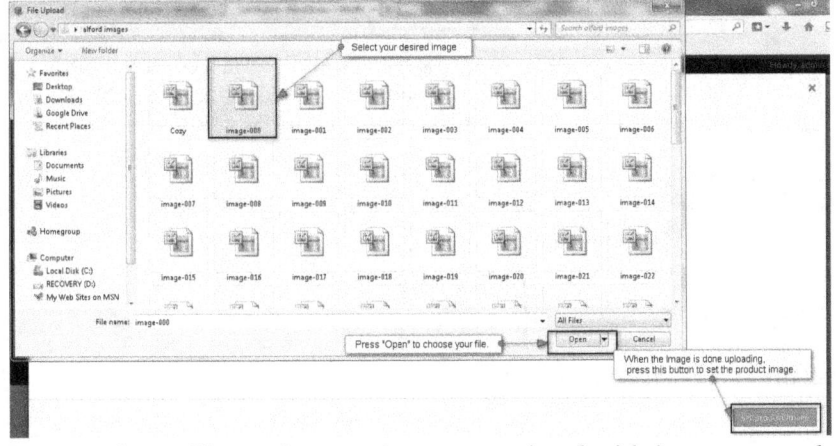

Your product will now have an image associated with it on your website.

Publish your product to your site

When you have finished **Adding your Product, Selecting Product Categories, Editing Fields,** and **Set Product Image**, your product is ready to be added. This process is called "Publishing."

The widget used for publishing to our site is on the right hand side of your WordPress administrator site.

The Publishing widget looks like this:

Here you can preview and publish your new products. You can also "save draft" to save the new product if you want to save your progress or if you want to make it available on a later day.

After selecting "Publish" your product is now available on your website

Editing Existing Products to WooCommerce

Sometimes, after you've added a product, you want to change product information, such as "Price" or availability.

First, log in to your WordPress page and navigate to your dashboard. Under "Products" you will find a link called "products."

You will see this screen:

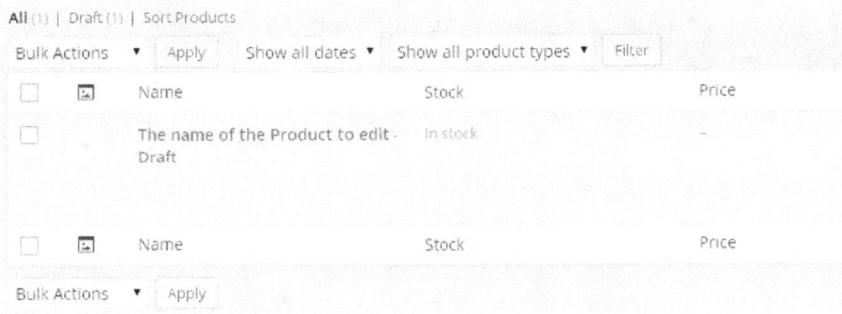

Click on the hyperlink of the product you wish to edit. You then will be navigated back to that product's screen.

You may now make any changes necessary to your product. The directions on editing the various product information pieces are *identical* to adding the product, except for the final, publication process.

When you are finished editing your product select "Update" to save the product changes.

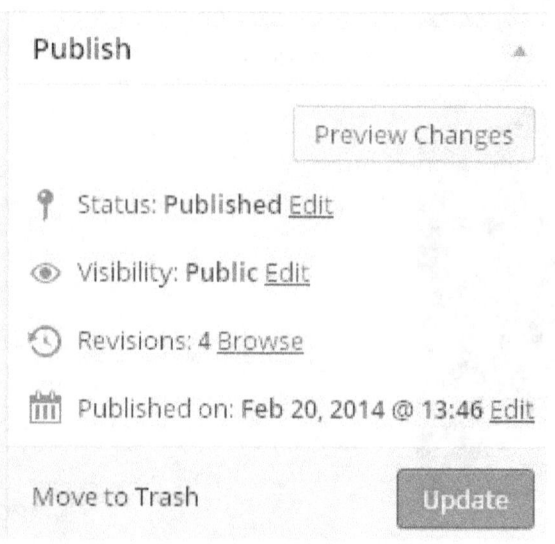

There! You can now manage your products through WooCommerce by adding, editing, and updating them through your WordPress administrator page.

Coupons and WooCommerce

Coupons can be a popular addition to any online store. Through WooCommerce, you can add a wide variety of coupons *and* edit their use. You can also add specific coupons with purchase of specific products and set limits on your coupons. Once your products are uploaded, you may want to add and edit coupons to your WooCommerce.

There are many options in WooCommerce for coupons, including Basic and Smart coupons.

Adding Coupons to your WooCommerce

Use these steps if you want to add or edit individual coupons in your WooCommerce.

To get started with WooCommerce Coupons, first navigate to WooCommerce in your Dashboard and select "Coupons."

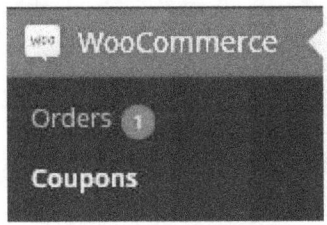

You will be navigated to the following screen:

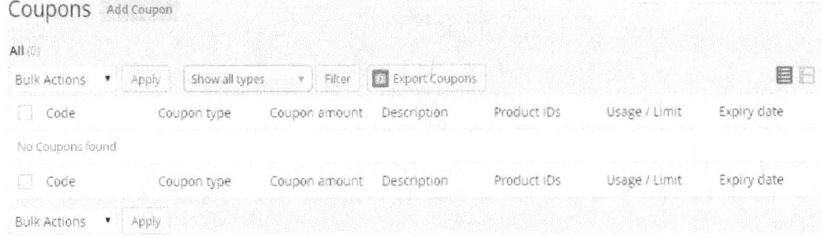

This is the home screen for all of your coupons. All of your coupons, even your expired ones, will show on this screen. You may delete coupons at any time, but they will remain in your WooCommerce system indefinitely.

To get started with creating your coupons, select "Add Coupon"

Add Coupon

The following screen has a wide variety of options and tabs. First, you will be directed to this screen:

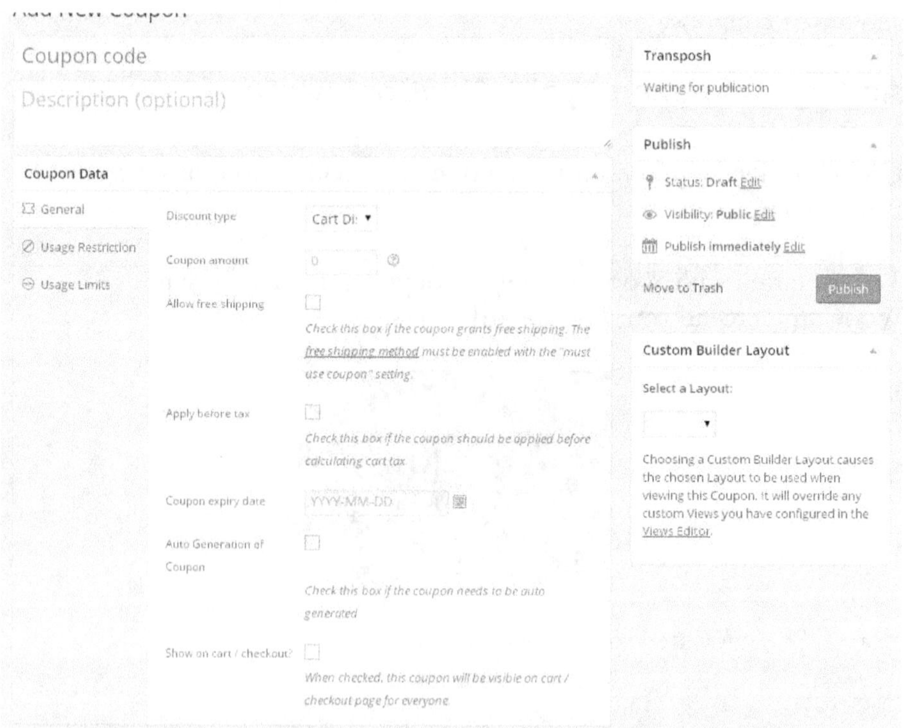

For our example, we're going to add a coupon that gives 50% off select products on Black Friday.
Under Coupon Code: Select the code you want your customers to use for the coupon,

In the Coupon Code box, enter the coupon code for your customers to use at checkout.

In the optional description, you may add a description of what the coupon is for.

BLKFRI

Black Friday 50% all Fan Favorites coupon!

Now we will navigate the three separate tabs on the screen to make sure the coupon does everything we need.

Editing the GENERAL Coupon Tab

The first thing you will see under the General tab is "Discount type."

Coupon Data

General | Discount type | Store C ▼
Usage Restriction | | Cart Discount
 | Coupon amount | Cart % Discount
Usage Limits | | Product Discount
 | Coupon expiry date | Product % Discount
 | | Store Credit / Gift Certificate

Selecting the proper discount type is highly important because this defines the type of coupon you will be giving your customers.

- *Cart Discount*- Discounts the entire order ($5 off whole order)
- *Cart % Discount*- Discounts a percentage off entire order (10% off valid orders)
- *Product Discount*- Coupon will only discount specific product ($3.00 off Bob's   Hair Gel)
- *Product % Discount*- Will take a percentage off only specified products
- *Store Credit/Gift Certificate*- Applies only in certain situations.

For our example, we will select "Product % Discount."

Next, enter the desired Dollar or percentage amount for the coupon. Note that adding the "%" or "$" is not necessary in this step.

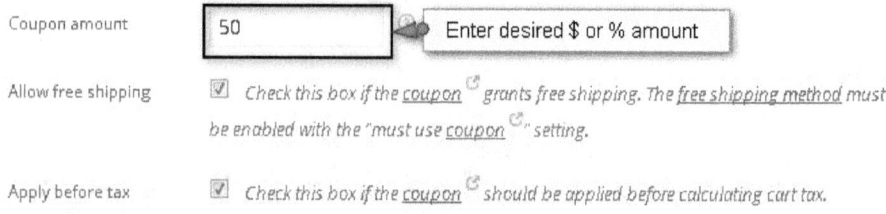

For our example, I have placed "50" in the box for a 50% Discount.

The next two boxes are fairly self-explanatory.

Check the first one if the coupon includes free shipping. (This one will only work if you have 'free Shipping method' available.)

Check the second if you want the coupon to include the pre-tax total of the item/cart discount.

The next box allows you to select the date the coupon expires.

To select the day you wish your coupon to expire, press the small "calendar" button by the box, The screen will show a calendar. Scroll to the proper date and select it to continue.

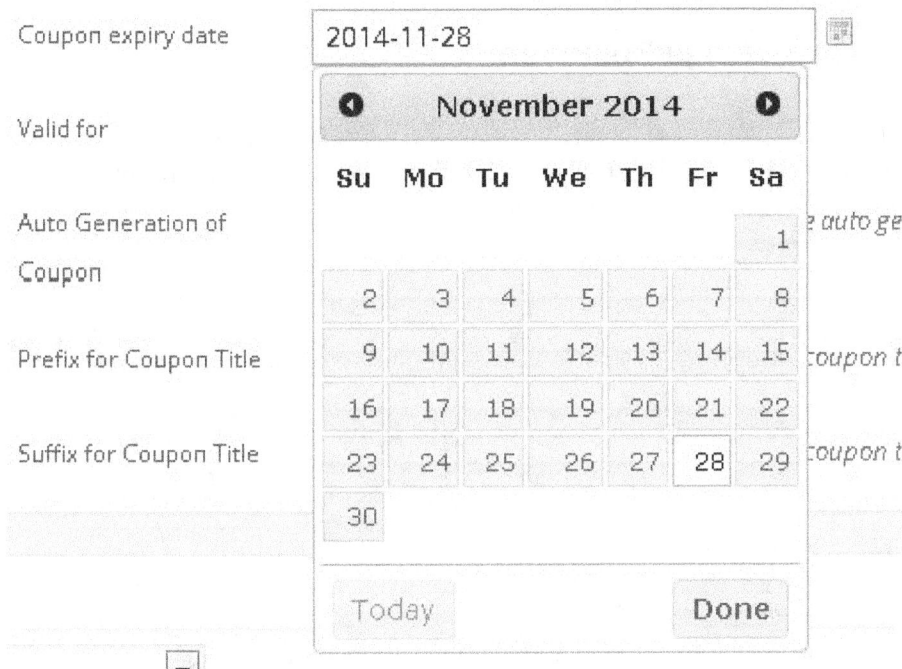

Now that the date is selected, you might decide to let the coupon "auto generate." You can do this by selecting "auto generate." This will give you the following box:

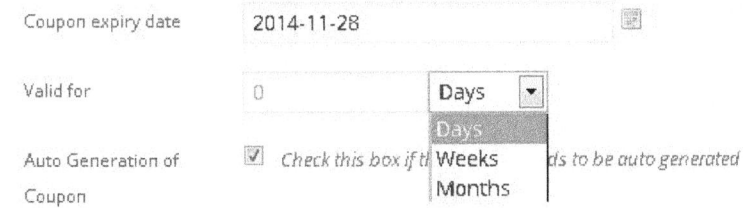

This will allow your coupon to expire in our chosen number of days, weeks, or months.

Once you've set "General information" navigate to Usage Restrictions to continue editing your coupon.

Coupon Usage Restrictions

Sometimes, when you create a coupon, you want to place restrictions upon its use. With the "Usage Restrictions" tab, you have a number of options you can use for that very purpose.

Here is the Usage restrictions Tab:

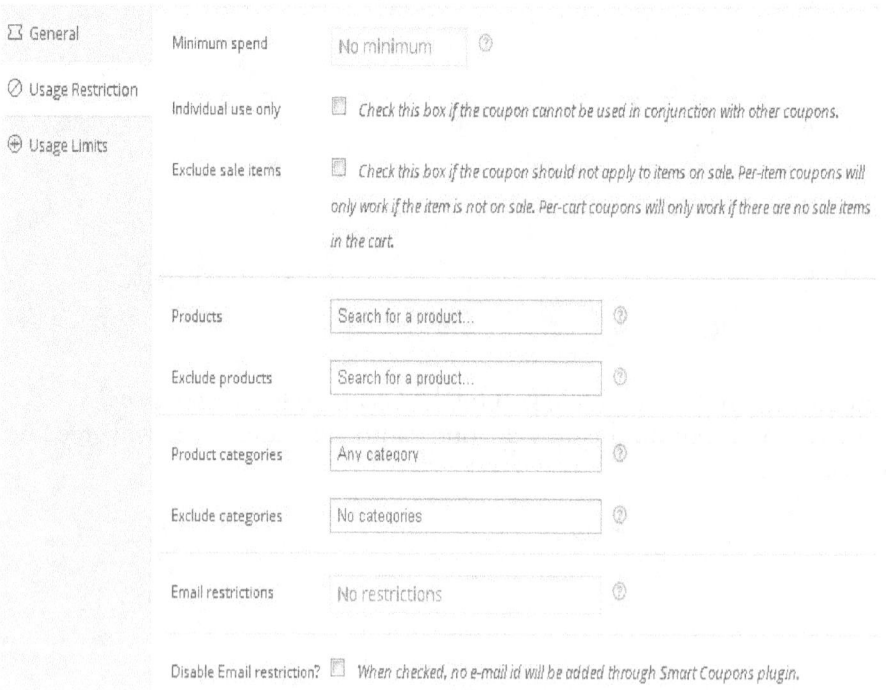

- *Minimum Spend*: The minimum your customer must spend to get the coupon
- *Individual use Only:* Check if you want this coupon cannot be combined with other coupons
- *Exclude Sale Items:* Check if you don't want the coupon to include sale items

For the next several boxes, simply type in the information you desire to use to limit the coupon.

- *Products:* Type in the name of product this coupon is intended for.

- *Exclude Products:* Type in name of specific products you wish to exclude from the coupon.
- Product Categories: Type in existing categories (see page 13) included in the coupon.
- *Exclude categories:* Type in existing categories that you do *not* want to sell with this coupon.
- *Email restrictions* will check the billing email against user database before applying coupons.
- *Disable Email restrictions:* When checked, no e-mail id will be added through Smart Coupons plugin.

Coupon Usage Limits

Sometimes, you want to limit the number of times a single customer can use a coupon *or* the total number of times the coupon can be used.
To do this, navigate to the "Usage Limits" tab of the coupon screen.

- *Usage limit per coupon:* Limits the use of the coupon to desired total uses.
- *Usage limit per user:* Each user will only be allowed to use the coupon desired number of times.

Once you've edited all the coupon information, you may publish your coupon.

Publishing your Coupon:

When you've finished designing your coupon, you may want to publish your coupon. WordPress *can* save your coupons as a draft. However, there are more options under the Publish Plugin.

First, navigate to the Publish Plugin on the right side of your WordPress administrator screen.

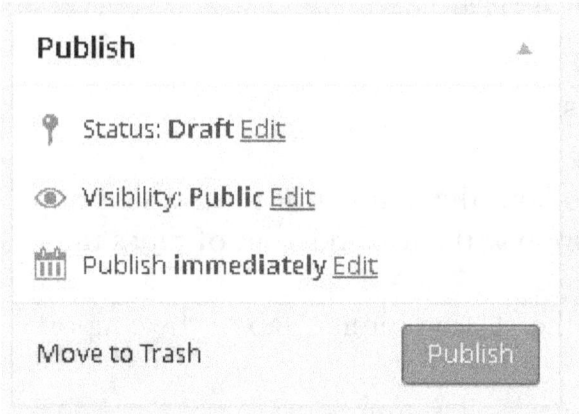

Under "Draft" you can select "Draft" or "Pending Review" on a drop-down menu.

Under "Visibility" you can choose to make the coupon private, public, or password protected.

Under Publish you can edit publishing day of the coupon. You may change the publication date by selecting the "edit" link.

Press the "Publish" button to continue. (note: If you've decided to postpone publishing for a later day, the button will say "Schedule.").

Delete Published Coupons

To delete published coupons, navigate back to your "Coupons" menu

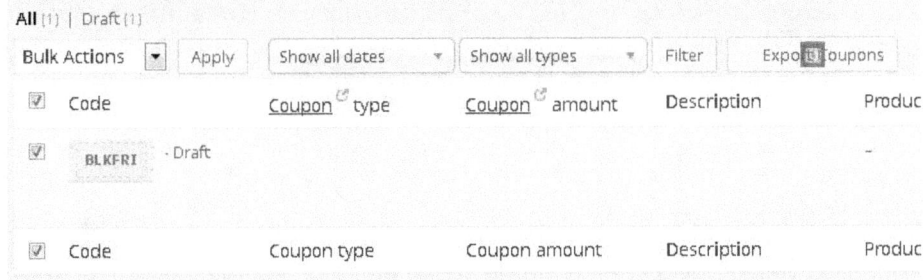

Enter a check next to your coupon's code in the box to its left.

Under the "Bulk Actions" dropdown menu, select "Move to Trash," then click "Apply."

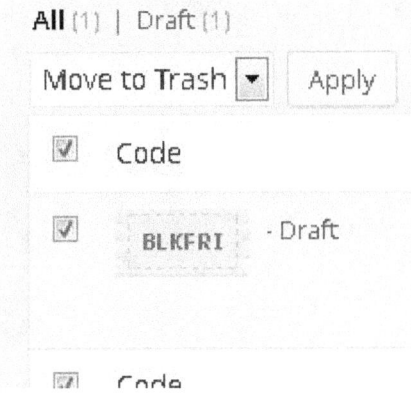

This will move the coupon to your trash bin:

To empty your Trash Bin, select the trash link.

This will navigate you to your Bin. Once you are there, select your coupon, find "delete permanently" in the dropdown menu, and hit "apply.

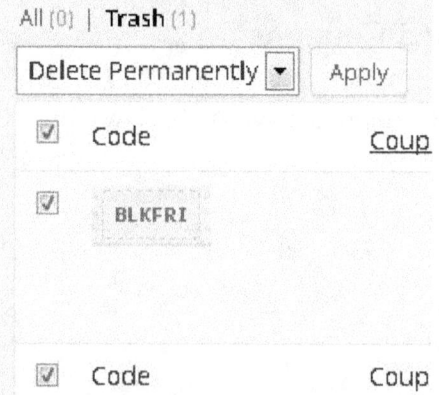

Your coupon will be permanently deleted.

Using WooCommerce Smart Coupons

WooCommerce Smart Coupon allows you to make multiple coupons at one time, edit them in a .csv file, and upload them in bulk to your site when you've finished.

You can also use Smart Coupon to send store credit to specific customers.

To get started using WooCommerce Smart Coupon, first log-in to your WordPress site, then navigate to "WooCommerce" on your dashboard. You will then select "Smart Coupon" on the menu.

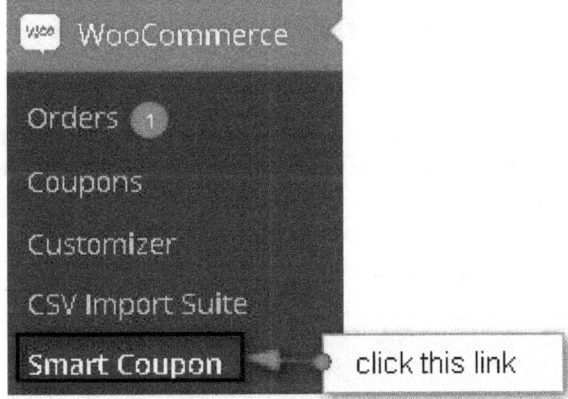

From here, you can begin generating coupons in WooCommerce Smart Coupon.

Generate Coupons in WooCommerce Smart Coupon

Under the "Generate Coupons Tab" you will find a number of options to help generate your coupons.

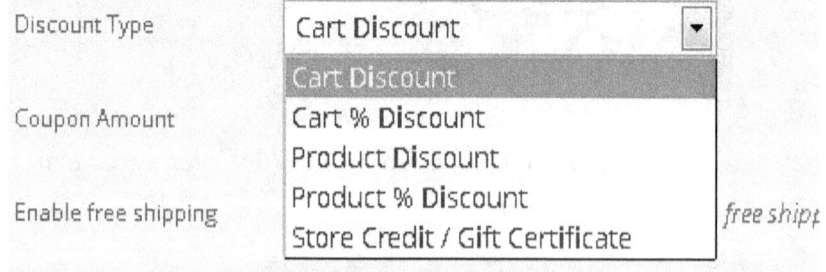

First, select the number of coupons you want to generate. The number you enter is the number of coupons you will generate.

Second, select the Discount type.

The discount types are as follows:

- *Cart Discount*- Discounts the entire order ($5 off whole order)
- *Cart % Discount*- Discounts a percentage off entire order (10% off valid orders)
- *Product Discount*- Coupon will only discount specific product ($3.00 off Bob's Hair Gel)
- *Product % Discount*- Will take a percentage off only specified products

Next, enter Coupon amount. Remember, there is no need to enter "$" or "%" because that variable was included under the discount type.

The next section of the **Generate Coupons** tab has a variety of check boxes. These boxes are fairly self-explanatory. Follow the instructions by the check boxes to determine if you wish to use those options.

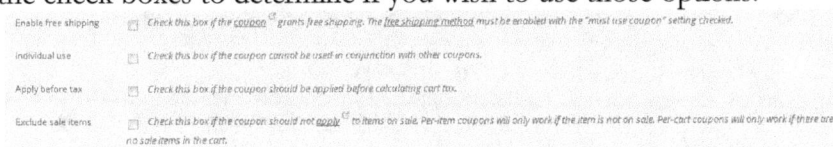

- Enable Free Shipping: Coupon Grants free shipping. (Free Shipping method must be aenabled)
- Individual Use: Coupon cannot be combined with other offers
- Apply before tax: applied before pre-tax total
- Exclude Sale items: if you do not want the coupon to apply to sale items.

The next box "minimum amount" determines how much the customer must spend before
they can use the coupon.

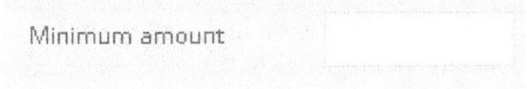

The next two boxes are for included and excluded products.

- Products: Type in the type in the name of desired products for this coupon. These products must be in the order for the coupon to apply.
- Exclude Products: The coupon will not apply to these products.

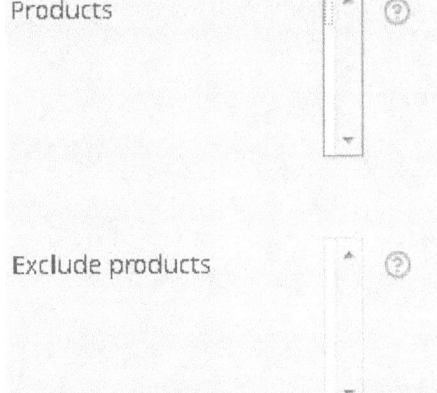

The next section will allow you to select the categories for your smart coupons. If you remember, categories help your customers by finding similar items. They can also be used to help include (or exclude) entire

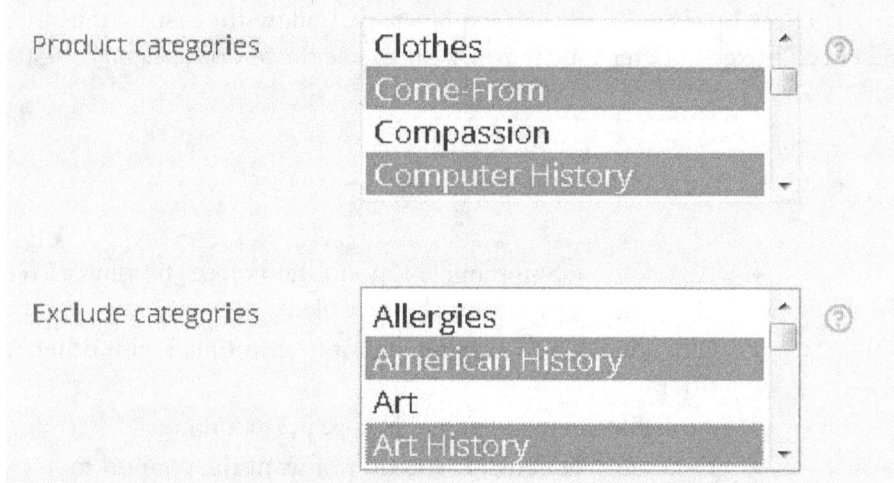

categories under a single coupon.

Notice that the boxes already include the categories for your products.

- *Product Categories:* Categories you want to include in the coupon. Products from these categories must be in the cart for the coupon to apply.
- *Exclude Categories:* These categories will not be included in the coupon. The products from these categories will not be included in the coupon.

To select multiple categories in either box, press "CTRL" on your keyboard and right click on your desired categories with your mouse.

The next section is fairly simple and sets restrictions on the coupon:

Email restrictions   ⑦

Usage limit

How many times this coupon ⬀ can be used before it is void.

Expiry date

The date this coupon ⬀ will expire   YYYY-MM-DD

- Email Restrictions: limits coupons to users with only certain email addresses. To use multiple emails, put a comma between each name. Each user will have a unique coupon code.
- Usage Limit: number of times this coupon can be used before void
- Expiry date: the day the coupon will expire.

The next section will allow you to add a prefix and suffix for your coupon code.

Prefix for Coupon Code

Suffix for Coupon Code

This will allow you to create a custom prefix or suffix to your coupon.

The next section is very important. The first check box says *"Generate only, do not add these coupons in WooCommerce. This will download a .CSV file which you can later import from* Import Coupons.*"*

☑
Generate only, do not add these coupons in WooCommerce. This will download a .CSV file which you can later import from
Import Coupons

Generate and Export .CSV file

If you select this box, it will generate the coupons in a .csv file. This will allow you to further edit your coupons through Excel or your .csv program.

If this is the option you want to use, check the box and press "Generate and Export .CSV file."

If you do not check this box, you have the option to email the imported coupon code to the respective customers/users.

E-mail imported coupon codes to respective customers/users.

Generate and Add to the Store

Whether or not you choose to check that box, if you want to generate the coupons instead of using a .csv file, select the "Generate and add to the store" button.

This will add your coupons to your store.

Import Coupons from CSV to WooCommerce

The next tab in Smart Coupons allows you to import a .csv file to create coupons in WooCommerce. This is how you will import a .csv created in the previous tab, if you chose to create the .csv instead of importing.

To get started importing your .csv, click on "Import coupons." Once you've done this, the following screen will appear.

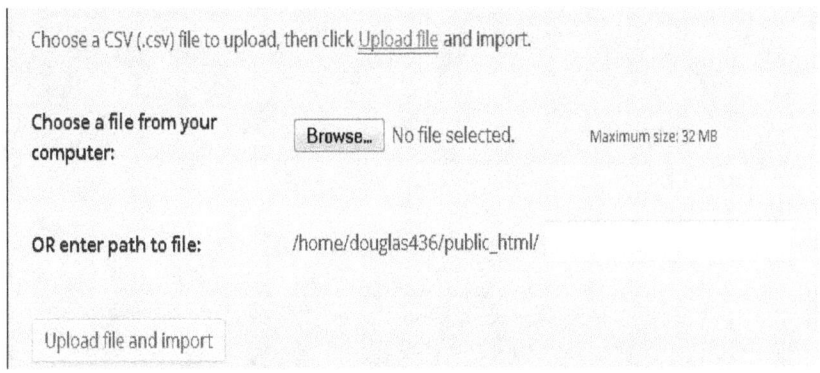

From here you have two options to upload your .csv file.

- For the first, you can click "browse" and navigate to your file.
- For the second, you can enter the path to your file

Once you've selected your file, click "Upload file and Import."

As soon as your .csv file uploads, your coupons ready to use.

Sending Store Credit through WooCommerce Smart Coupons

Occasionally, you will want to send store credit to your customers. This is a very simple process.

First, select the "Store Credit" tab under the Smart Coupons menu.

Generate Coupons	Import Coupons	Send Store Credit

Send Store Credit / Gift Card

*Click "Send" to send Store Credit / Gift Card. *All field are compulsary.*

Email ID *

Coupon Amount *   0.00

Send

In the first box, enter the email id of the customer you wish to give store credit to. Next, enter coupon amount. They will get an email confirming their store credit and it will be in their account, ready to use on their next visit.

Managing Orders in WooCommerce

Once your customers have placed orders in their WooCommerce cart, you can examine the orders made. This allows you to do a number of things.

To examine orders made on WooCommerce, first Log in to your WordPress account.

Next, navigate to your dashboard under "WooCommerce" and find the "Orders" option.

The little blue number next to "orders" shows there is an order in the queue.

You will be sent to the following screen:

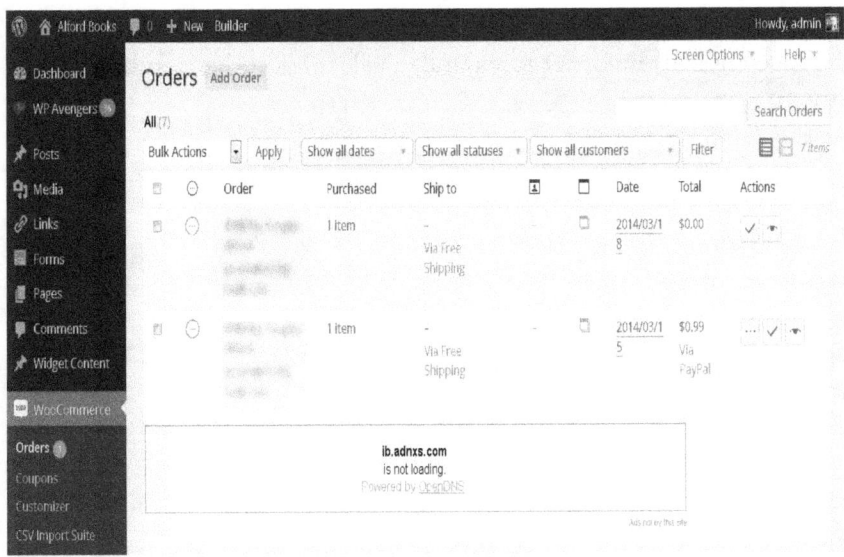

This screen allows you to see all your orders. The Orders are arranged by order number, not alphabetically.

To manage an order, select its entry in the order screen. Each order has a marker beside it to mark its status:

Orders that are processing

Orders that are on hold

Cancelled orders

Once you've chosen the order to examine, select it's order number on the order menu.

Examining the Order Screen

The Order Screen has a lot of different sections. Here is an overview:

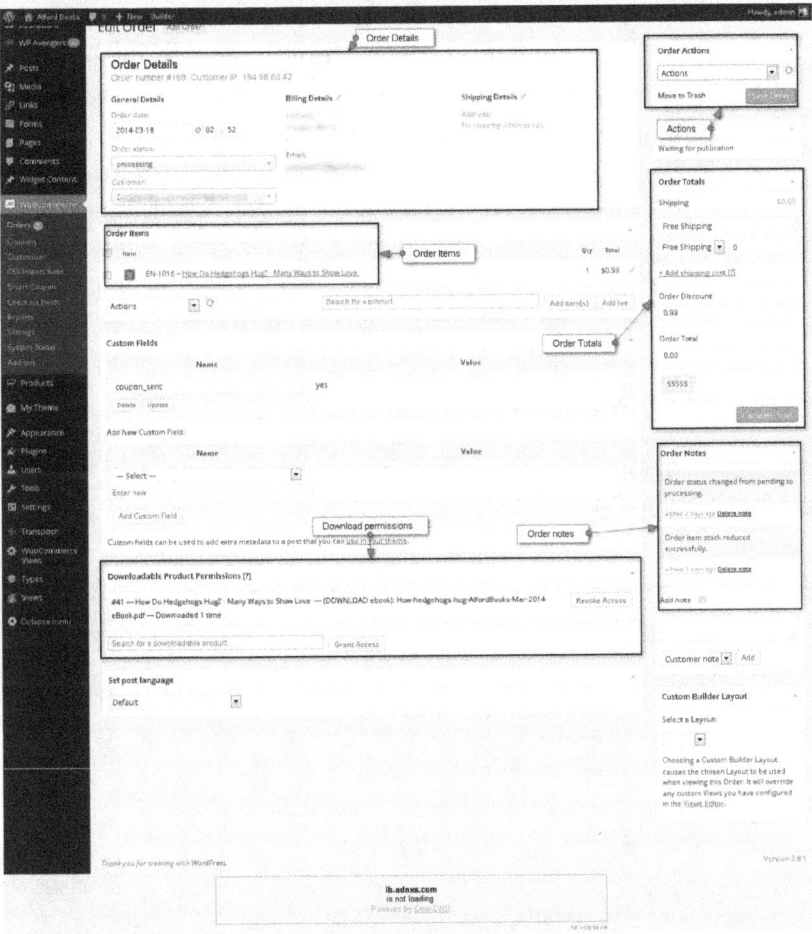

- *Order Details:* shows the details of the order: customer name, email address, billing and shipping address, order status.
- *Order Items:* Items in the customer order.
- *Actions:* your actions made on the order.
- *Order Totals:* how much the customer spent on the order.
- *Order notes:* marks any adjustments you have made to the order and a place to leave notes on customer communication.
- *Download permissions:* If product is downloadable, this shows the permission to download and gives you a place to revoke download access. For this workbook, we will not worry about download permissions.

Order Details

From the Order Details portion of the screen, you can examine the specific information about the order.

Here you can see specific information about the order, including date the order was placed, customer email, order status, customer, billing and shipping address.

From the Order Status drop-down, you can change the status of the order.
The different statuses are displayed in the picture below.

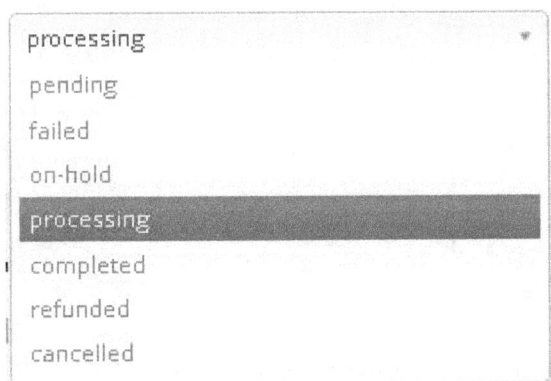

Use this drop-down to change the status of the order, if necessary.

The Customer drop-down will show a list of your customers.

Order Items:

This section will show you items ordered in this particular order.

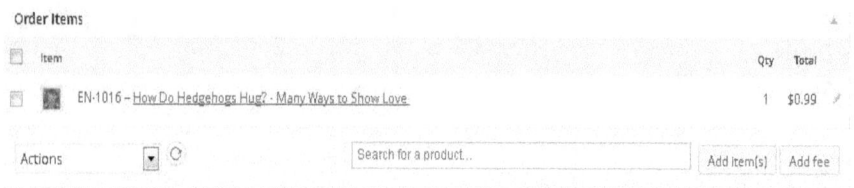

As you can see, this order includes only one item: SKU EN-1016, *How do Hedgehogs Hug?*
If the order had multiple items, they would all be displayed on this screen.

Order Actions:

This drop-down menu allows you to resend order emails to the customer.

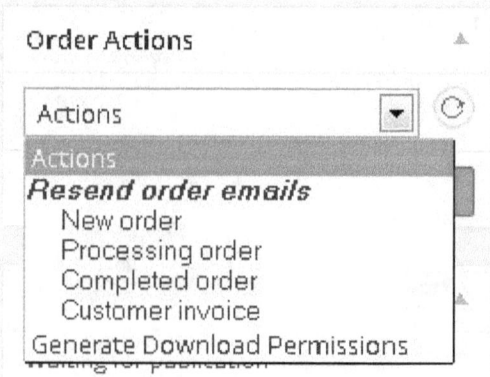

It allows you to make a new order, show order processing, complete order, generate customer invoice, and generate download permissions for your customer orders. This will be most handy if you are manually creating an order for your customers.

Order Totals

The Order Totals menu will show you everything about the order total.

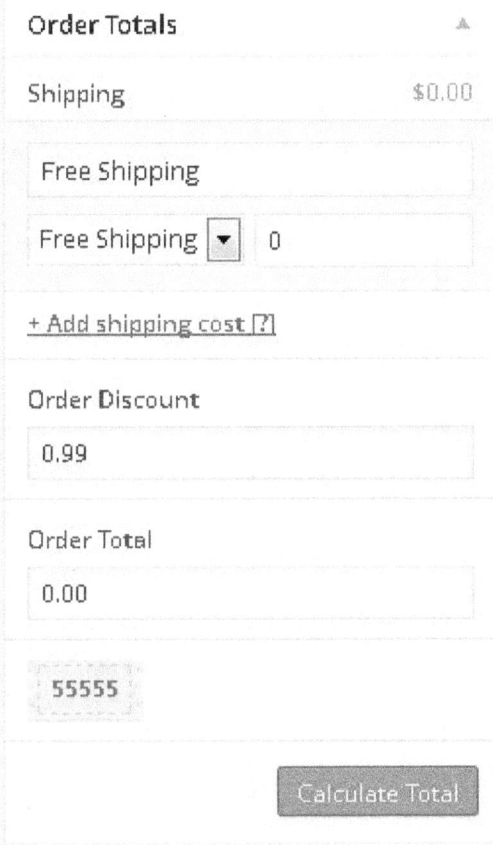

From here, you can see shipping costs, free shipping information, order discounts, and the order totals.

If any coupons were applied, you will see the coupon applied as well.

Order notes

This section allows you to mark any adjustments made to the order and leave notes on customer communication.

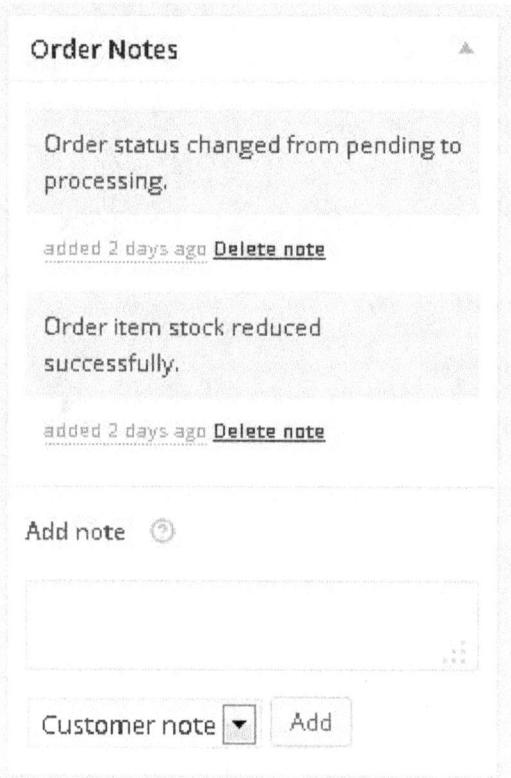

As you can see, for this order, item stock was reduced and the order status was changed to processing.

To add a note, simply type your note in the box and select "add." Using the drop-down menu, you can mark notes as "customer note" and "private note."

This can be very helpful if you've had any communication about the order with the customer or if you've had to cancel/refund the order.

Managing Reports in WooCommerce

One final aspect about WooCommerce involves reports. WooCommerce Reports allow you to track sales and customers. With Reports, you can track sales by Product, Customer and date as well as tracking coupons. All tracking can be done for the following time periods: this year, this month, last 7 days, or a custom date range.

You can also use Reports to manage your customer database and your stock/inventory.

To get started with WooCommerce reports, first log on to your WordPress Administrator page. Second, navigate down your WordPress Dashboard and find "WooCommerce." The Option for "Reports" is under the WooCommerce menu.

You will be navigated to this screen:

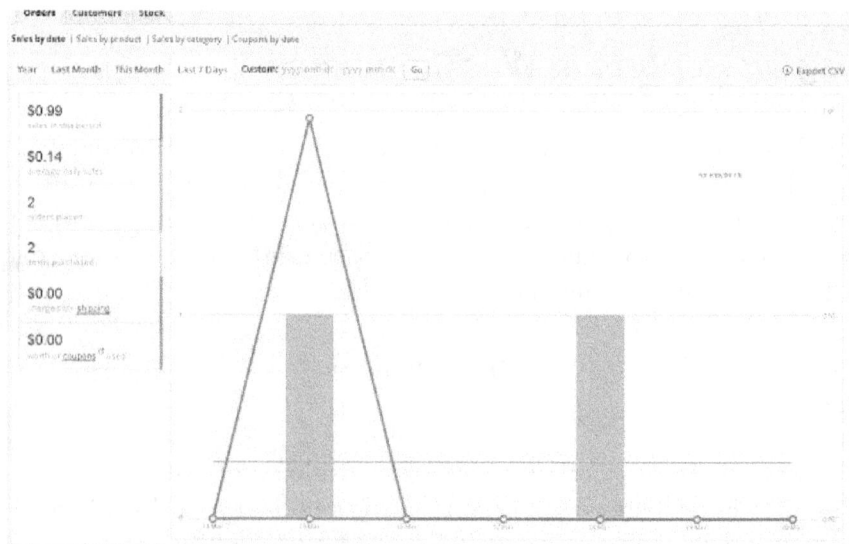

From here you may begin viewing your reports

Tracking your sales with WooCommerce Sales Reports.

To Track your sales with WooCommerce Sales Reports, first you must log on to your WordPress Administration page, find WooCommerce, and open the reports tab.

The Default screen for WooCommerce Reports shows the last seven days of sales. On the top of the screen, you will find the options for your reports:

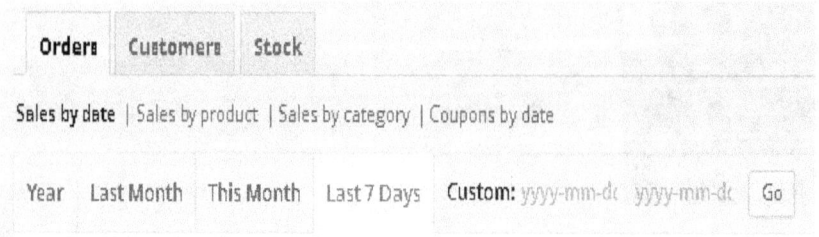

Stay under the "orders" tab.

To view your desired report, click on the report type and select the desired date range.

Report Types:

Sales By Date: Sales by date defaults to show you the last seven days, all products sold.
The "Sales by Date" report will break down the sales your WooCommerce has tracked in a specified date range. The Default is the last seven days:

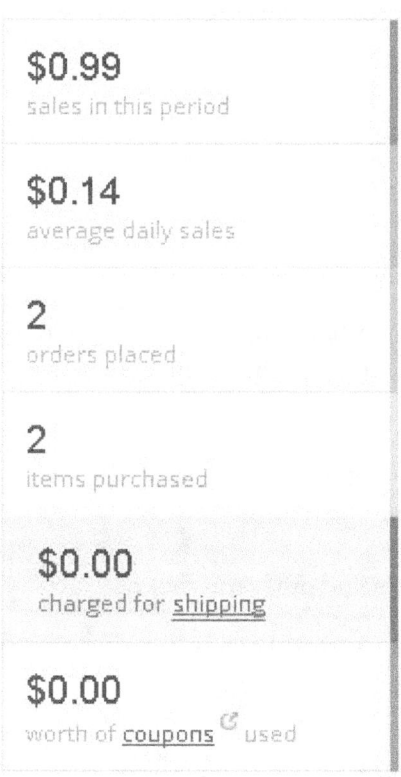

This widget, on the left side of the screen, shows how many orders have been placed, how many items purchased, total sales, average daily sales, shipping cost and coupons used in the specified date range. Highlighting a specific section of this data will highlight the information in the line graph that follows immediately to the right on the report page.

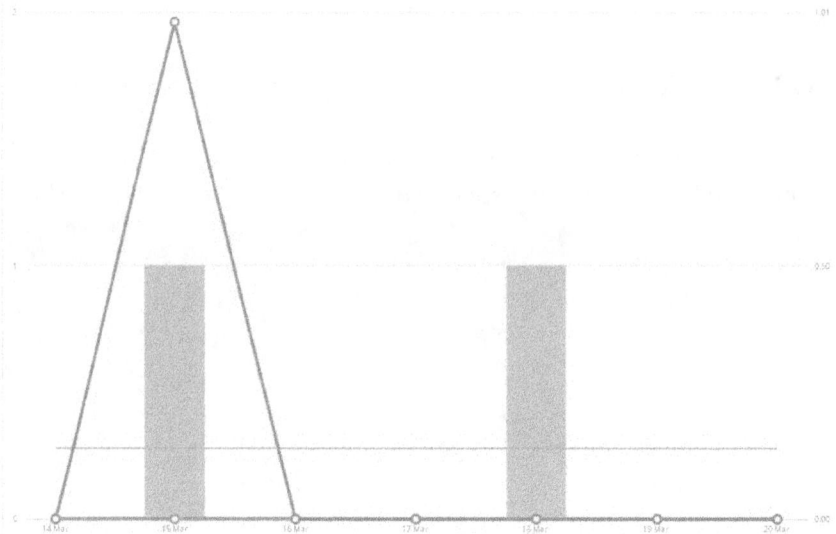

To change from "Last Seven Days" to any other date range, select one of the default date range options (Year, Last Month, This Month) or select your desired date range.

For instance, if you want to track sales over a three month period First, find the "Custom" date range section.

Click your mouse over the first set of dates and enter the first date you want to search for.

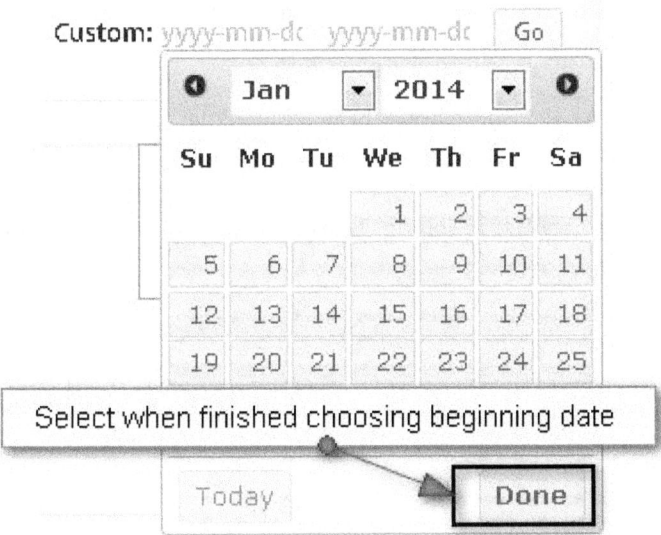

You can use the drop-down menu to select the month and year, then click on the proper date to select the first date in the sales period. Next, follow the same instructions with the next custom date range for the end date.

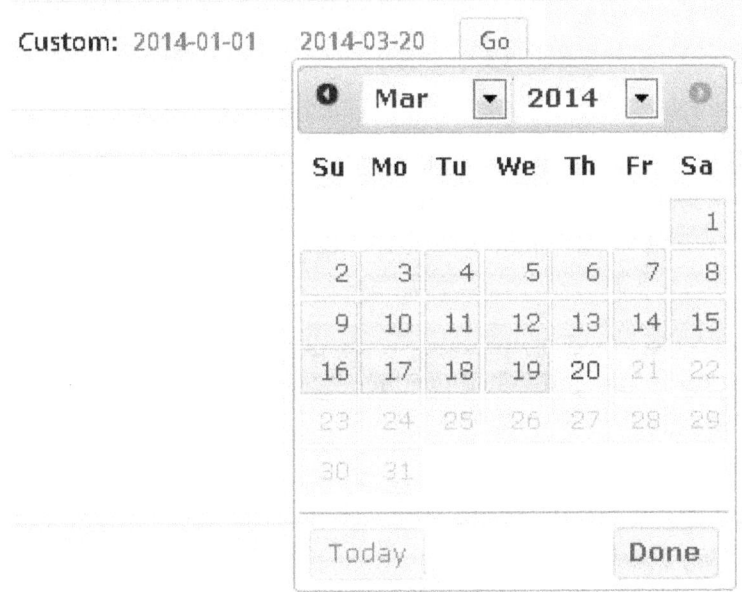

Once you've selected your two dates, press "Go."

This will generate the report for a three-month period or any other custom date range.

Sales by Product: Sales by Product shows how a particular product or products are selling over the specified date range

To track how a particular product is selling, first go into reports and select "Sales by product."

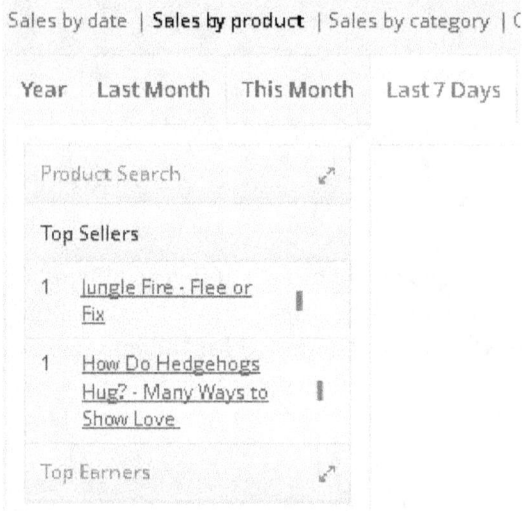

There is not a line graph available for this information. Instead, you will find your top sellers on a menu to the left. Click on any product to see its sales information. For this example, we will examine the first product on the list.

Once you've selected the product, you will see the line graph and information for the individual product.

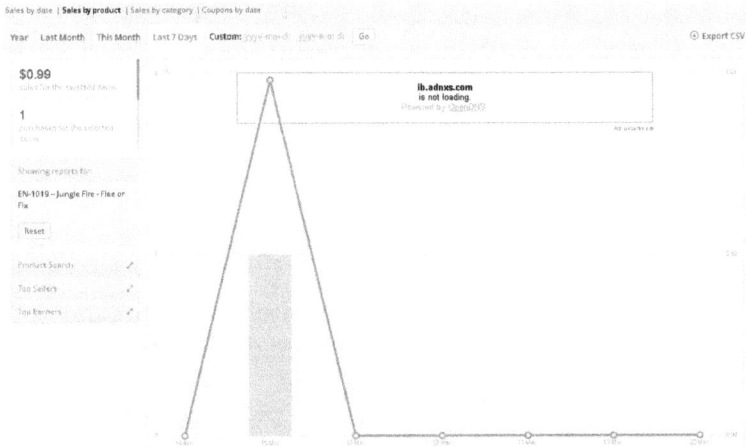

Just like with the "Sales by Date" only option, if you select an area on the left-hand menu, it will highlight on the line graph.

If you look at the left hand menu, you will find more options have appeared.
From this screen, you can search for products, find your top sellers and top earners.

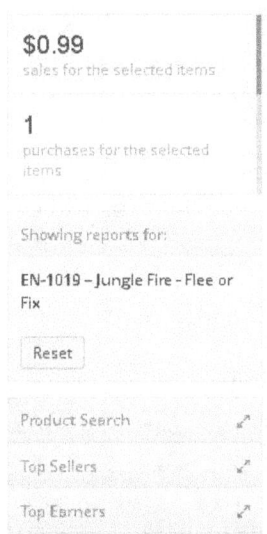

To search by any of the parameters, simply click on the blue double arrow symbol by the parameter and enter product name or click on the link available.

Product Search

Search for a product...

Show

For this option, type the name of the product you are looking for and press "show."

Top Earners

Top Sellers

$0.99 Jungle Fire - Flee or Fix

1   Jungle Fire - Flee or Fix

$0.99 How Do Hedgehogs Hug? - Many Ways to Show Love

1   How Do Hedgehogs Hug? - Many Ways to Show Love

To search either by "Top Seller" or "Top Earner" simply click the hyperlink of the product's name.

Sales by Category: Sales by Category is *nearly* identical to Sales by Product, only you are looking for entire categories of products instead of individual ones.

To track an individual category, select the "sales by category" hyperlink in the Reports toolbar.

A dropdown menu will appear:

You can select multiple categories by holding "CTRL" and right-clicking the categories with your pointer.
Once you've selected the categories, the dropdown will close.

This by category search will find three categories to display. Select "Show" to complete the category search.

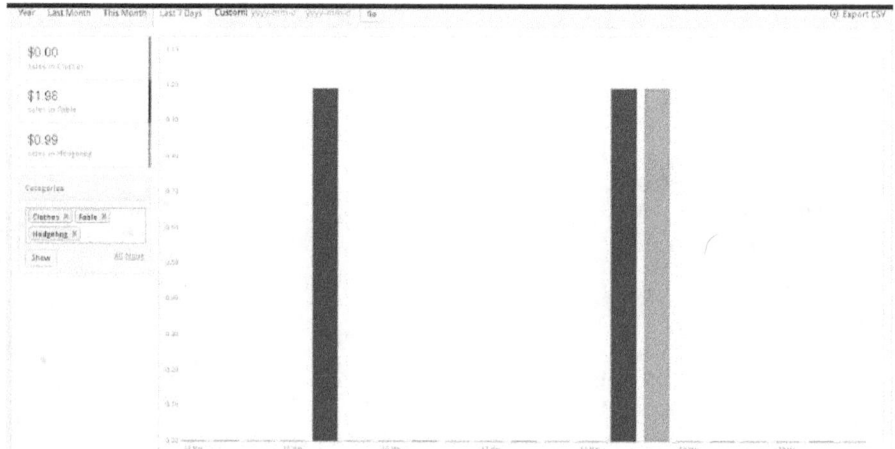

This time, you will see a bar graph comparing sales by categories over the selected date range.

Just like with the sales by date and sales by product, if you click on a selection in the left-hand box, those options will be highlighted in the graph.

Coupons by Date:

This option will allow you to track the popularity of your coupons. Again, you can change the date range using the same steps outlined in "Sales by date."

First, click on the "Coupons by Date" link. A bar graph will appear, and on the left you will see an information box. Just like with the other reports, clicking on a selected piece of datain the information box will allow you to highlight that data on the graph:

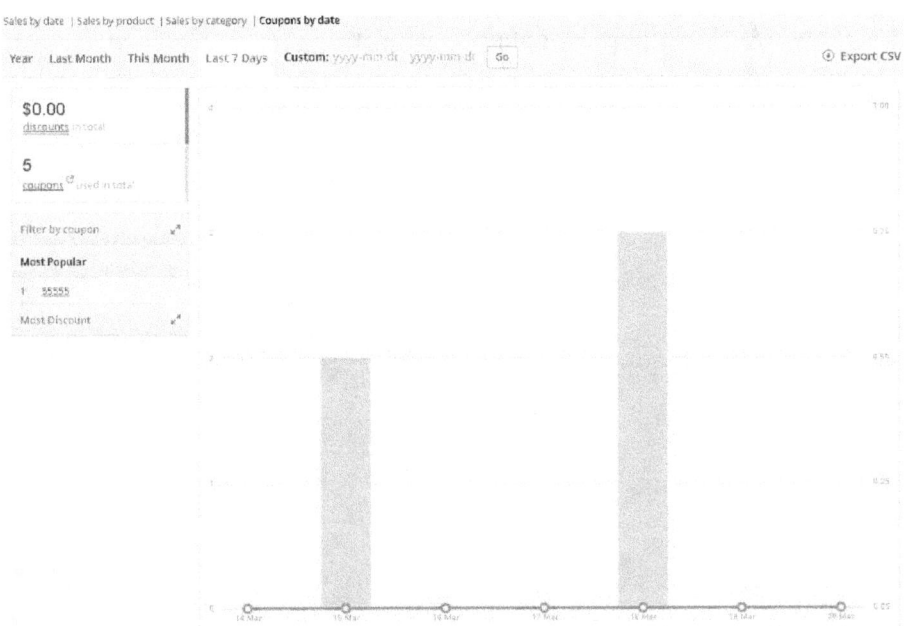

In the information box, you will see:

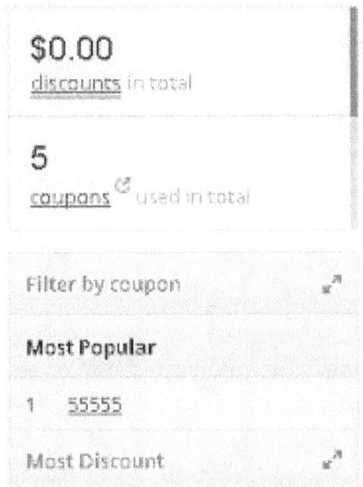

- The total number of discounts.
- Total number of coupons.
- A "filter by coupon" widget

- A "Most popular coupon" widget.

Tracking your WooCommerce Customers in Reports

You can use reports to track your sales. But, you can also use your WooCommerce to track your customers. First, you must navigate to your WooCommerce by logging into your WordPress Account, finding the "WooCommerce" widget, then finding Reports. Next, you will select the "Customer" tab.

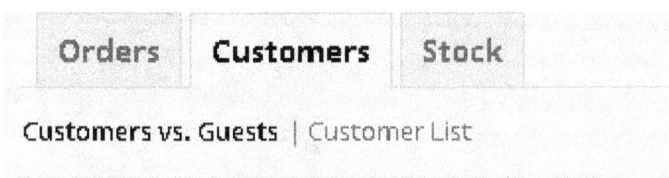

You will see two different options.

Customers vs. Guests

Under Customers vs. Guests, you can see a detailed chart of sales made to "customers" tracks sales made to registered customers vs. "guests" (people who do not have an existing account through your WooCommerce site).

Just like with the order reports, you can sort customer vs. guests orders by a wide range of date categories. Follow the same steps that you would follow under **Sales by Date** (p. 45).

Your Customers vs. Guests report will look like this:

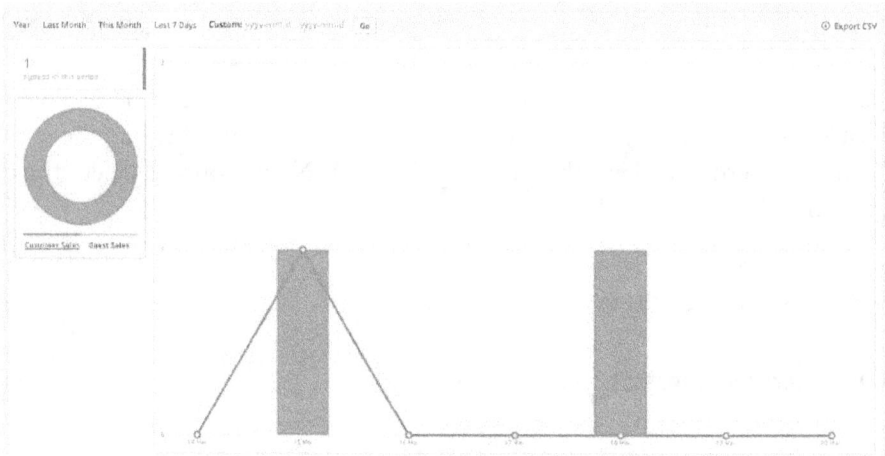

The information box on the left is much like other report information boxes, if you click on a data set, it will be highlighted in the graph in the center of the page.

The information bar shows some interesting information:

Sign ups in this period shows the number of new customers signed up in the specified date range.

The circular chart, or "Doughnut" chart shows the number of Customer vs. Guest sales. The solid color of the example shows that there are no guest sales in the given date range.

Customer List

The Customer List tab will highlight all of your customers and their email addresses. This can be used to generate an email list and can be highly helpful if you need to show that you have an existing customer database for credit or investment purposes.

To see the customer list, first select the "Customer List" hyperlink under the "Customer" tab.

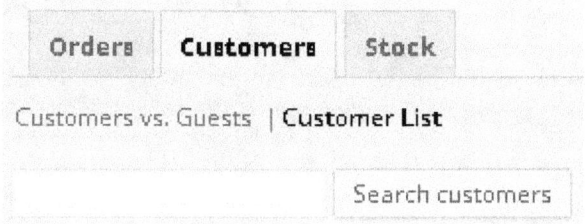

A similar list will pop up:

Name (Last, First)	Username	Email	Location	Orders	Spent	Last order	Actions
			United States (US)	0	$0.00	#168 – March 18, 2014	
Name (Last, First)	Username	Email	Location	Orders	Spent	Last order	Actions

This list only has a single name, but if you have multiple customers, they will all appear in this list.

You can also search for individual customers by name under the "Search Customers" tab at the top of your screen.

Information you will find in your customer list:

- Name
- Username
- Email
- Location
- Number of orders
- Money spent
- Last order (number and date)

Examining your Stock and Inventory in WooCommerce Reports

Thorough WooCommerce Reports, you can examine your inventory as well as sales and customers. First, you must navigate to your WooCommerce by logging into your WordPress Account, finding the "WooCommerce" widget, then finding Reports. Next, you will select the "Stock" tab.

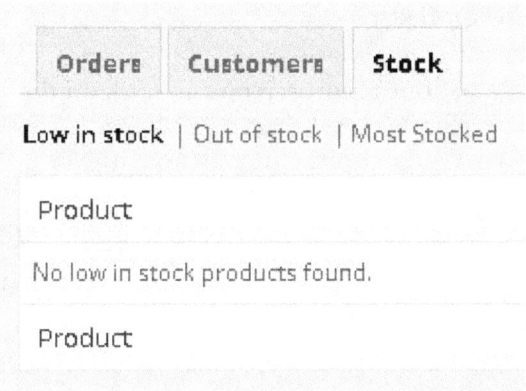

There are three hyperlinks:

- Low in stock: Will show items you are low on in inventory
- Out of Stock: Items you are out of in inventory
- Most stocked: Will show what you have in inventory/what is the most stocked.

To use any of these options, click on the hyperlink.

Note: if your store is made of all downloadable products, this option will not be necessary and you may never use this report.

Exporting your WooCommerce Reports to a .CSV file

Once you've generated your reports, you might want to export them to a .csv file. This can be done for a number of reasons, for instance to maintain a hardcopy record or to provide a copy of your sales or client list for a business meeting.

It does not matter if you are exporting your ORDERS or CUSTOMER reports, because the process is identical in both situations. For our example, we will export the CUSTOMER report.

First, go to the far right hand side of your report screen and click on the "Export CSV" link.

A windows Dialog box will appear on your screen.

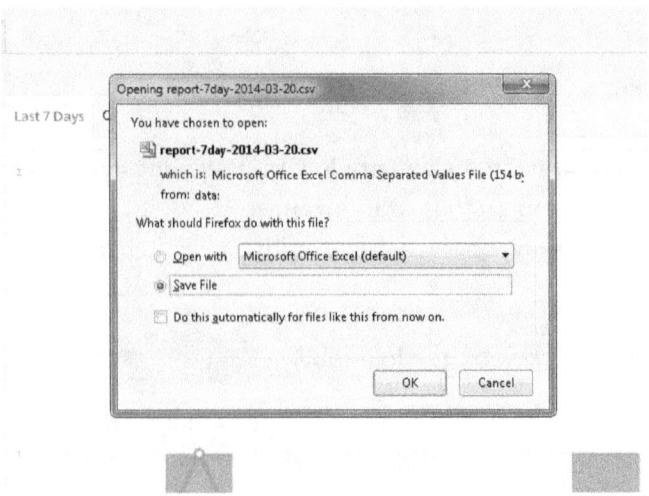

Always select "Save File" so that your file is saved on your computer and press "Ok."

The file will now save in your "Downloads" folder (or in your computer's default download location) under the title specified in the dialog box.

For More Assistance with WooCommerce and Web Design:

Desert Sea Design's team of expert web designers work with WooCommerce on a regular basis, and are more than happy to help you set up your web store, organize your products, and help set up and test product coupons.

Simply Contact us:
Via Phone: 623-536-3297
Or
Email: info@desertseadesign.com

About the Authors

Mandy Oviatt has a Master's of the Arts in History from the University of Houston, Clear Lake. She is the head writer for Desert Sea Design and a disabled Veteran of the U.S. Army.

Lyle Dillie is an Interdisciplinary Artist, Iraqi War Veteran, and proud husband and father of three boys. Along with Nikki Rowe, Lyle is currently the Co-Owner of Desert Sea Design a Web, Graphic and Print Company based out of Avondale, AZ. He graduated, Summa Cum Laude, with an Interdisciplinary Art Degree at Arizona State University.